"UNWRITTEN LAW."

AN ADDRESS

DELIVERED BEFORE THE

PHI BETA KAPPA SOCIETY
OF HARVARD UNIVERSITY,

AT CAMBRIDGE, MASSACHUSETTS,

June 28, 1877,

BY

THOMAS FRANCIS BAYARD,
OF DELAWARE.

BOSTON:
A. WILLIAMS AND COMPANY.
1877.

US 2185.45.10

From Estate of
Edward Everett Hale

UNIVERSITY PRESS: WELCH, BIGELOW, & CO.,
CAMBRIDGE.

ADDRESS.

GENTLEMEN OF THE PHI BETA KAPPA:—

THE invitation to address you, with which for a second time I have been honored, found me in the midst of the abundant and engrossing duties of a member of one of the houses of the legislative branch of the National Government, and you may not be surprised to find that

> "almost thence my nature is subdued
> To what it works in — like the dyer's hand,"

and that the thoughts which, on this occasion, I propose to submit for your consideration, relate to the government of our common country, — the great American commonwealth in whose citizenship, with its legacies of honor and lofty example, its present privileges and responsibilities, and its hopes for a future of glorious fulfilment, we all rejoice.

In other countries the discussion of the topics of law and government might be properly addressed only to those exceptional bodies or classes of citizens upon whom the duty and control of public affairs devolve, and who, under their system, relieve the general body of inhabitants from all responsibility for the consideration and adjustment of such dry and difficult questions.

Not so here. In America we have embarked our political fortunes, and staked all our hopes of good government, upon the capacity of a free and intelligent people to govern themselves by the institution and maintenance of wise and just laws, as means to attain the great ends of liberty, tranquillity, and happiness, the independence and elevation of the minds and characters of the people.

It is at once evident that individual independence in thought and expression is peculiarly needed, under our majority rule, and is, at the same time, more endangered than where a less number of rulers is to be consulted. The absence of political ranks or classes removes the barriers to the uninterrupted roll of the great wave of public opinion which is so apt to submerge and bear down opposition from individuals.

Therefore, as the number of minds to be reached and consulted is greater in America than elsewhere, the task of government is greatly increased in its difficulties by reason of the popular form it assumes here; and in congratulating ourselves upon our privileges, let us not be unmindful of the duties that go daily hand in hand with them, and which justice imposes upon all who would earn the right to enjoy them.

It is a great truth that liberty must rest upon a moral rather than a political basis, and has its real security not in charters or statutes, but in the peace and happiness, the independence and elevation of mind, which it brings to such as can truly comprehend and enjoy its delights, which, once tasted, create a healthy thirst which nothing but pure fountains can satisfy.

By it men are developed in mind and soul; it increases and encourages activity in both; and, founded, as in our American system, upon the profound assurrance and trust that the good elements in human nature are more powerful than the evil, and are continually gaining on them, the result is, that in an increased activity the preponderance of what is good will increase, and that society will advance with an accession of virtue, of national power, freedom, and independence.

Upon nothing less lofty is founded our theory of American liberty, and we have sought its security in a government of laws, as the basis of peace and order which their execution guarantees. It is true that liberty is held under government, but the liberty of opinion keeps government itself in subjection to its duty.

> "This is true liberty, when free-born men
> Having t' advise the public, may speak free:
> Which he who can and will, deserves high praise,
> Who neither can nor will, may hold his peace.
> What can be juster in a state than this?"

It is by law alone that the fixed and durable possession is created, which is called property. Men exercise foresight, labor, and economy, and the fruits of all are secured by law; industry creates and law preserves; before the law there was no property; take away the law and property ceases.

In this presence I need say nothing of the manifest duty and necessity of the constant subordination of the will of individuals to the established laws, because it is so manifest that no government could stand were the general will permitted to be counteracted by individual opinion or caprice. Life in society is impossible without such mutual relations and such a common bond, and social order would inevitably be dissolved if every man declined a practical acquiescence in any political regulation he did not personally approve.

While the duty of submission is founded in principles in force under every government of laws, under our American system are superadded the additional persuasion and obligation to obedience to the laws, that they are mainly the creation of those who are to be governed by them, and the demands of a common security are strengthened by the appeal of good faith. And this makes obedience to law the honorable duty of the American citizen, and elevates his obedience by the dignity of the motive in which it originates. Political indifference must be fatal to a republic; and we have no less authority than Dr. Arnold, the influence of whose high nature and great faculties has so blessed his own and other countries, for saying that "the highest earthly desire of the refined mind is to take an active share in the great work of government."

And now by your leave I will submit some reflections upon what in my opinion constitutes our best reliance for the honorable and successful government of this great republic, under the institutions established by our forefathers.

The real scope and practical dominion of mere legislative enactments — the statute-law of the land over the happiness, welfare, and character of the people — has often seemed to me exaggerated and unduly magnified in the mind of the average legislator, who flies hastily to pass ill-considered statutes as a panacea for the ills of state, and the be-all and the end-all of good government.

The consequence is a medley of laws, scarcely to be called a system, for stability is seldom permitted, and in it no broad and wholesome principle of government can be traced.

It is a garment not woven, but made up of shreds and patches, without continuity of idea visible in any part, until the opportunities I have had (I will not say enjoyed) for closely watching its practical working would lead me to believe the most beneficial legislation to-day would be statutes of repeal, bills for necessary appropriations, and resolutions of adjournment.

Is it not a radical error to suppose that by statute-laws you can prescribe a course of human conduct?

A man's course of conduct includes the great body of his actions, — his *habitual* action, not his occasional acts, — and involves his motives at every stage.

Statutes must speak in general terms, and address themselves, not to one nor a few, but to all. When, therefore, we consider the vast variety of man's undertakings, the infinite details of his daily occupations, the infinite variety of motive that actuates him, how can it be said that law can prescribe a course of conduct?

Laws are the result of legislative vigilance, and, in fact, do little more than prescribe negative duties; performance they can compel in but a very limited class of actions, and their chief force is in prohibition. They give and can give no suggestion of either morality, religion, justice, or good feeling, and act mainly by way of restriction upon some of the tendencies of mankind.

They amount to little more than a restraint upon the actions of individuals, and that upon a very limited number of their acts, and possibly point out a formal execution of a few others; and this idea is fundamental to the whole structure of statute-laws.

It is only in a very small and insignificant part of

the domain of human nature that law can be applied. I find my thoughts best stated by an English writer, Mr. Pierson, who, in a late work, says: "All that the law does in its substantial provisions is to restrain. It commands nothing except in the subsidiary machinery. It restrains only a few things. Like the good demon who attended Socrates, it may prevent one going wrong, but cannot prompt one to do right. It does not teach a man what to do, but only what to avoid, or how to accomplish a few things in a formal way. It does not supply the motive-power, or direct the course of the journey; it only erects a finger-post here and there. To say, then, that the law prescribes or enforces a course of conduct is, as nearly as possible, the converse of what it professes to do. An individual may do all that the law requires, or rather avoid all that the law prohibits; and yet, if he knew nothing but what the law told him, he would scarcely survive a week. The great majority of the actions of each individual proceed from motives far beyond the reach of the law, and such as the law can neither give nor take away."

Hence, it is the most difficult of all problems in the science of government to determine when and where and how it is wise to interfere by the authority of law with the motives which are usually called the natural motives of men, — as it is evident that the force of laws, and their value, depend almost entirely upon the assent or the consent with which those to whom they are addressed shall meet them.

The law cannot prescribe the performance of the virtues; but it is addressed to the reason, and seeks to influence human action, by and through the will, by presenting an alternative to each prohibited act. More than thus appealing to the reason and presenting an alternative the law cannot do! There can be no decree for the specific performance of legal duties. The horse may be brought to the water, but something over and above law is required to make him drink!

It is this consciousness of the limited power of the law which should instruct us, that it must be addressed to reason, and command the assent of all reasonable minds; otherwise, interminable discontent and confusion must ensue.

Having thus stated the impossibility of commanding a course of human action by the instrumentality of written laws, let me now remind you how infinitely wider is the sphere, and more permeating and constant the influence, of the UNWRITTEN LAW; by which I do not mean *lex non scripta*, the common law of custom, acquiescence, and judicial decisions, but the *great moral law* "written," as Coke said, "with the finger of God on the heart of man." "The law of laws, truly and properly to all mankind fundamental, the beginning and the end of all government," as Milton called it.

Whatever influence written laws obtain, they gather from the secret forces of nature which have been considered in their framing, and the failure of so many laws passed in disregard of natural laws should instruct us in this great truth.

Persecutions for opinion's sake have always increased heresy; protection laws have injured trade; poor-laws have increased poverty, and usury laws have raised the rate of interest. This is common experience. I am sensible of the difficulty of providing a definition for the *unwritten law*, which cannot be reduced to formulation or codification. Human government can never be subjected to geometrical exactness, and can only be measured by approximations. Form and method will do only for things of form and method.

There is, after all, a unanimity of the entire human race in the great rules of duty and the fundamental principles of morals; the general sympathies of mankind flow together and a general judgment is arrived at. There are certain principles to which all nations do homage, and the majesty and authority of virtue are derived from this common consent.

One proof of this is to be found in the proverbs common to all nations, and their great antiquity.

In this way the unwritten law is formed and accepted, and being formed in the hearts of men is hearkened unto and obeyed in every emotion and in every act, and the attempt to escape its influence is vain. "You may pitchfork nature out, but she will ever return," is as true to-day as when Horace wrote it.

The case now comes to my mind of a brave gentleman who obeyed the unwritten law of patriotic duty, and left his home here in New England for the battlefields of Virginia. There he was wounded, almost unto death, and so mutilated that amputation became necessary to save his life. He submitted to it, but wrote to his betrothed, telling her to what a mere wreck and remnant of humanity he had been reduced, and offering to release her from her engagement. Quickly the reply sped, "If enough of your body is left to hold your soul I will be your wife."

Could a statute "command the course of conduct" of these two beings, or cause your hearts and mine to swell, as they do now, at this simple recital?

This is what Dr. Johnson meant when he wrote for Goldsmith the lines in "The Traveller":—

> "How small, of all that human hearts endure,
> That part that laws or kings can cause or cure."

Wise rulers will carefully endeavor to frame their laws in accordance with a just public opinion, not public clamor, but settled opinion and sentiment; for they may rest assured that otherwise, directly or indirectly, defeat awaits them.

In the history of the world how many laws have been reduced to "dead letters" by this disregard, and have fallen into contempt, of which lawlessness is the necessary outcome.

"The laws of my country are written in blood," said Sir Samuel Romilly, at the commencement of his honorable and prolonged career of legal reformation in England. And well might he say so. The punishment of death was awarded, not only for every description of the *crimen falsi*, but for the least serious offences against property, for picking pockets, pilfering five shillings from a shop, or forty shillings from a dwelling-house. Offences against the revenue, depredations upon bleaching-gounds, secretion of goods by bankrupts, tumultuous assembling of the people and not dispersing in one hour after proclamation by a single magistrate, forgery, were all in the long list of capital felonies, and, as a consequence, the *unwritten law* of human nature came into conflict with such statutes. They were not in unison with human feelings, and could not be executed.

In countless ways they were evaded and defeated by what Sir William Blackstone (certainly no legal reformer) called "pious perjuries."

Parties injured, concealed the commission of the offence, or refused to prosecute or testify. The judges, by strained constructions of the statutes, aided acquittals, and juries were quick to render verdicts based upon the failure of the prosecution in the sheerest technicalities of proof.

The penalty was felt to be unduly severe, and society forgot its horror of the crime in its greater horror of the excessive punishment, and sympathy for the offender.

A jeweller prosecuted a lad for the theft of a silver cup above the value of five shillings. The penalty for the offence was death. There was no doubt of the theft, but the jury refused to find the value of the cup to be above five shillings. The prosecutor exclaimed, "Why, my Lord, the design of that cup was worth more than five shillings." "Heaven forbid," said his Lordship, "that a fellow-creature should be hanged for a design." Thus are sanguinary statutes wiped away by the gentleness of humanity.

The dark and disgraceful history of Catholic disabilities under the statutes of William III. and the Protestant succession (the repeal of which is so near our own day) is full of illustrations.

By one of these laws any Roman Catholic having a horse over the value of £5, could be deprived of it at any time upon tender of that sum. On one occasion, observing a fine animal at the smithy, one Major Sirr inquired the name of the owner, and learning that he was a Roman Catholic gentleman of the neighborhood, tendered £5 to the groom, and took away the horse.

The indignant owner brought an action of trover, and the jury of Protestants (for none others were then qualified), restrained by the law as to the value of the horse, yet returned a verdict for the plaintiff of fifty guineas for the *halter*, which had inadvertently been taken also.

Such cases should teach us that the influence of laws is just in proportion to their approach to our reason and to the springs of human action.

Can the retention upon the statute-book of a law be

justified which, under a system of popular government like ours, excludes from the jury-box more than ninety per centum of the men of property and intelligence in a community?

And yet it is a sad fact that under section 820 of the Revised Statutes of the United States, it is to-day a cause of disqualification and challenge to any grand or petit juror in the courts of the United States " ever to have served in the Rebellion, or given it aid or comfort, or to have given any assistance directly or indirectly, or *anything whatever*, to any one or for the use of any one whom the giver knew to have been engaged in arms against the United States."

Under this we witness in fifteen States of the Union the great body of native white citizens excluded from all share in the execution of the laws as jurors, and the strange anomaly can daily be witnessed of marshals selecting and summoning juries, of district attorneys addressing them, and judges instructing them, when neither judge, prosecutor, nor marshal would be qualified to serve as a juryman.

We have had an Attorney-General of the United States so disqualified, and other Cabinet officers and officials of various ranks.

The complex and delicate nature of the machinery of our Government, and the duplex character of American citizenship under it, increase the need of the *unwritten* law. Witness the conflict necessarily arising from the jurisdiction, and variant legislation upon the same and most important classes of subjects in thirty-eight independent States, with no forum in common to adjust their discrepancies.

We need it to create *a sentiment of nationality* among

all the people of all the States, which can never be the product of any body of statutes nor alterations in the phraseology of the Constitution.

As I have said, written laws can do little more than restrain men, and for the force which creates and compels action we must look to the unwritten law.

The government of the Union makes us in many and important respects one people. In war we are one people, in making peace one people. In commercial regulations we are one and the same people, and for all these and many other objects the government of the United States is our only government. To it is committed the control of all external affairs of the Nation, and those internal affairs which affect the States *generally*, or in their relations to each other. Chief Justice Taney said: "For all the great purposes for which the Federal Government was formed, we are one people with one common country. We are all citizens of the United States, with the rights which belong to citizens of all the States as members of the Union." But as to those matters which are completely within a particular State, which do not affect other States, such as the regulation of its police, its domestic trade, civil rights, the rights of persons and property, and that immense mass of legislation which embraces everything within its territory excepting the enumerated powers delegated to the General Government, the power of the State is exclusive and supreme, is acknowledged and is essential to the perfect working of our complex system of free government.

In this "divided sovereignty," as Daniel Webster termed it, independence and harmony are required for the State governments, that they may the better subserve the purpose of cherishing and protecting the "respective families of this great republic," as they were so happily styled by Mr. Justice Johnson.

The State governments are the true pillars upon which rest our national system; it is upon their rectitude and strength that the government of the Union must rely for its support. Any construction of the Constitution or policy of administration that invades their independence in any of those matters, not intrusted to the General Government, is a blow at the entire system and can be dealt only in blindness or treachery.

It is not now my purpose to enter the debatable ground of State and Federal jurisdiction, but always, so far as I may, to aid in the creation of that spirit of harmony and conciliation between the two which should characterize the administration of public power, and which, after all, is the one thing needful for its maintenance.

A little reflection will serve to satisfy any reasonable mind of the impossibility of conducting a Government such as this, based upon the underlying principle of voluntary support by its citizens, in any other mode than local self-government in the several States.

We must rely upon the capacity of our people to govern themselves, and to obtain this capacity they must be exercised in the faculties requisite for the end. Local self-government is the true and only school of the American citizen, in which he starts with the essential equality, — equality of opportunity, and retains ever the greatest of opportunities, — the opportunity of amendment.

By his very failures and mistakes he is chastened and instructed, and the virtues of self-reliance, independence, and sturdy perseverance are all brought into action to aid in the necessary education of his faculties.

The separation of the domain of the federal and the State governments not only subserves liberty by distributing power, and preventing its dangerous and undue concentration, but the spheres of official power being thus limited, the places under either government may be safely committed to men of moderate acquirement and capacity.

It was an important object with the founders of our system by a separation of the jurisdictions, and a subdivision and limitation of powers, not only to curb ambition, but also to enable men of average ability and moderate education to engage usefully and creditably in the public service.

Our system is to be maintained by keeping these objects in view, and carefully restricting State and Federal authority to their respective jurisdictions, and sustaining each in its sphere, never overlooking the need of a spirit of harmony and co-operation between the two.

A glance at the enormous area of our territory; the extreme differences of climate and temperature; of soil; of production; of occupation, habits, customs, creeds; and, above all, of the diversities of origin and races of the people by whom it is inhabited, will suffice to satisfy any one that the idea of providing a single code of laws which should relate to all the objects of domestic government, and under which such a nation could reasonably expect to live in tranquillity, is simply preposterous.

The alleged exercise of Federal powers in a spirit of local favoritism has already, in our history, proved a serious ground of discontent and dissension among the States.

A resolute maintenance of their rights, and a disposition to resent injustice or encroachment, is one of the characteristics of a free people, and attests their sense of the value of the privileges in question.

We should all foster a strenuous and generous rivalry in the paths of industry and activity between the States of our Union; and, to insure that the spirit of jealousy and animosity should not arise between them, we should adopt, as the safest rule of administration, a systematic limitation of the exercise of Federal functions to such a minimum as will be consistent with the unembarrassed performance of all its necessary duties and the thorough maintenance of its just powers and prerogatives, leaving to the several States unfettered control of their own domestic concerns.

I care not how worthy or learned a body of men may be, they will never be able to frame laws to control the daily lives of a community of whose tastes, habits, and occupations they are ignorant.

The first object of a law should be to bring it into harmony with the people; for this a study of their temper and habits, their traditions and associations, their virtues and infirmities, are all requisite; and to this, one who does not live among them and sympathize with them can never attain.

At Madrid a Spanish king prohibited the wearing of round hats, which being a disguise became a cover for assassination. The people revolted, and the law could not be carried out. He then ordered the public executioners should wear them, and no one else could be found to do so.

Government is a moral and not a mathematical science, and one of its greatest forces is sympathy, and sympathy fixed by habit becomes affection.

"I knew a very wise man," said Fletcher, of Saloun, "that believed if a man were permitted to make all the ballads, he need not care who should make the laws, of a nation."

We need the force of an *unwritten law* to establish in the hearts and minds of the American people a sense of the dignity and impartiality of the government of the Union; a general and habitual reverence for its justice, and a spirit of proud obedience to its laws, not mere slavish and sullen submission to its power.

To aid in the establishment of such a sentiment we need the recognition of the equality of the States in our constitutional scheme, a public opinion that shall discourage and prevent assaults upon the credit or good repute of any portion of the Union, and a popular resentment that shall visit any man or body of men exhibiting hostility and malevolence towards his fellow-countrymen.

In other words, we need an invigorated and realizing sense of the value of the Union to the happiness, security, and honor of all its members, so that perceiving their freedom they will use it to strengthen the government whose institutions are the source of their freedom, that they may realize the truth of the exclamation of Charles James Fox,

"Liberty is order, Liberty is strength."

that laws of repression may be regarded with distrust in the knowledge that public virtue owes more to freedom than to jealousy and restraint.

A nation may be overthrown in other modes than by force. Its institutions may be wrecked by incompetence and ignorance, it may be undermined by dishonesty and falsehood, or may crumble in the dry rot of corruption and demoralization.

If the limits so carefully assigned by the Constitution to the Government of the Union are to be disregarded in favor of the theory of a paternal government, and a constant system of intermeddling with the local and domestic affairs of the States is to be sanctioned, soon will follow a habit of reliance upon it in all cases, and we may naturally look for a system of national aid to local improvements, and all the numberless enterprises which should be left to individual and local energy and resources will be prosecuted under the patronage of the Federal treasury, until every canal, railroad, and other improvement will be expected to be built under the fostering care of the General Government.

Political organizations will then be arrayed like storming parties for assault on the public treasury, and national bankruptcy cannot long be averted.

Politics will become little more than systems of skilfully organized plunder, and the abuses will grow with what they feed upon.

From such a theory nothing but vicious administration can result. It will create taxation and expenditure, and attract to its support the venal. It will foster violence and disorder, and the timid will seek it for protection. It will create immorality, and the pious will seek its power to counteract the very wrongs it has generated. There has been enough, and more than enough, in the actual history of our own times to prove that what I have suggested has had practical illustration, and the distress we witness to-day throughout the country is largely attributable to such causes.

There are economic problems that now confront us which call for all the statesmanship, good sense, and good feeling we can muster for their solution.

In the legal profession is to be found a class of laborious and painstaking men known as "case-hunters," whose acute but narrow minds seem never able to perceive the *principle* which runs through cases, and which once apprehended serves to reduce them to orderly classification.

In medicine there is a class of practitioners who give little heed to anything but an accumulation of remedies, which constitute their only reliance, and which they collect with great assiduity and apply with equal alacrity,— a pet drug or potion for the symptoms they are called to relieve, but who are never occupied in reverently considering the great laws of health, a limited perception of which would be so much more useful in preventing the seeds of disease from being planted and bearing their fatal harvest.

In matters political we have a kindred class of huckstering statesmen who, for every disorder of the body politic, have ready at hand a disabling statute, a penalty or test-oath ready for administration to the disobedient or disaffected, whose idea of government is "a combat by decrees, an invasion by constables and a spoliation by judges,"— small-minded men whose little souls cannot comprehend the calmer wisdom that, perceiving the great laws of human sympathy, render discontent and disorder short-lived or impossible by removing or avoiding the *causes* for their existence.

It is to the hearts of the American people that I turn with most confidence, and in the force of the *unwritten laws* my chief hopes are reposed.

I wish I could bring to the minds of those who hear me now the spirit and meaning of a scene which took place two or three years ago in one of the Southern States, whither I had gone to urge in friendly counsel the rejection of some false and dangerous suggestions in relation to our national finance, which were being introduced and recommended disingenuously and mischievously by political agents from other parts of the country.

In the utter impoverishment of an agricultural people, suffering from a disorganized system of labor, prostration of industries, and an abolition of the only banking facilities upon which they had been accustomed to rely, it is scarcely to be wondered that any promise of immediate relief, even the shallow and mocking cry of "more money," should have been hailed with delight.

It seemed to me then to be my duty to warn those fellow-countrymen of ours against not only the false economies of such doctrines, but to develop the danger to our national credit, and the assault upon the Government itself, that lay concealed within the propositions of renewed "inflation" and "convertible bonds."

One evening after a pleasant dinner, and in all the freedom of social assembly, these topics were debated in a room filled with men of whom I was almost the only one who had not "worn the gray" from 1861 to 1865.

The discussion was vigorous, — first the economic and finally the patriotic side of the question, — and to my appeals on this point there was but a chilly response, for it was in the days when military menace unhappily still survived as a political force of administration in the affairs of some of the States.

Finally I said, "Gentlemen, you are all very positive, and unwilling to accept my views, but I think I know how to control you, and despite your strong language can find means to obtain your submission."

There was no response for a moment; an atmosphere of resistance seemed to fill the room, and in the eyes around me shone a light of defiance. Then one of the party asked, with some severity of manner, "Pray, sir, *how* do you propose to manage us so easily and compel our submission?"

I said, "I would give you power to do right, and then I would defy you to betray the trust. You, yourselves, should be your conquerors."

There were few men in that room who had not faced death in battle, and many bore the scars of conflict on their persons; but as I looked around the angry light of resentment had passed from their eyes, which were not unmoistened by a generous emotion, and I was left the victor on that field.

Who that has tested man's nature fairly but must admit that the spark of our higher origin lingers in the human breast, and that our better nature will almost always respond to the appealing voice of higher motive and more generous emotion?

Do you remember how Dickens, with his wonderful eye for human nature and his extraordinary power of painting its likeness in caricature, tells us, in the history of "Nicholas Nickleby," of the necessity of allowing the weaker side to prevail in order to satisfy public demand in matters theatrical?

Nicholas is introduced to Mr. Vincent Crummles, who is superintending the rehearsal of a combat with broadswords between his two sons, the Masters Crummles, in the character of a tall sailor and a short sailor respectively.

"There's a picture," said Mr. Crummles, motioning Nicholas not to advance and spoil it. "The little one has him; if the big one does n't knock under in three seconds he is a dead man. Do it again, boys."

The two combatants went to work afresh, and chopped away until the swords emitted a shower of sparks; and the exciting struggle finally ended when the short sailor (who was the moral character evidently, for he always had the best of it) made a violent demonstration and closed with the tall sailor, who, after a few unavailing struggles, went down and expired in great torture as the short sailor put his foot upon his breast, and bored a hole in him through and through.

"What do you think of that, sir?" inquired Mr. Crummles.

"Very good, indeed, — capital!" answered Nicholas.

"You won't see such boys as those very often, I think," said Mr. Crummles.

Nicholas assented, observing that, if they were a little better match —

"Match!" cried Mr. Crummles.

"I mean if they were a little more of a size," said Nicholas, explaining himself.

"Size!" repeated Mr. Crummles; "why, it's the essence of the combat that there should be a foot or two between them. How are you to get up the sympathies of the audience in a legitimate manner if there is n't a little man contending against a big one? — unless there's at least five to one, and we have n't hands enough for that business in our company."

"I see," replied Nicholas. "I beg your pardon. It did n't occur to me, I confess."

"*It's the main point*," said Mr. Crummles.

Grotesque as is the picture, who will deny its underlying truth, or fail, in the midst of their smiles, to recognize a touch of that nature " which makes the whole world kin"?

One of the purest and highest thinkers of our day, Sir Henry Taylor, says:—

> "Generous sorrows and high purposes
> Make the dumb speak. Ye orators, note that,
> That in the workshop of your head weave words."

We often find the philosophy of social life in Bulwer, who tells us grave truths dressed in the garb of poesy and romance, and none the less delightful or valuable for that.

He has drawn, in "My Novel," a charming portrait of a gentleman in whom a large knowledge of the world has not created distrust in mankind, or disbelief in the better side of human nature.

Harley L'Estrange has sought the Marchesa di Negra, who has taken up a book from the table.

"Have you seen this work?"

Harley glanced at the title-page. "To be sure I have, and I know the author."

"I envy you that honor. I should like also to know one who has discovered to me deeps in my own heart which I had never explored."

"Charming Marchesa, if the book has done this, believe me, I have formed no over-flattering estimate of your nature; for the charm of the work is but its simple appeal to good and generous emotions, and it can charm none in whom those emotions exist not."

"Nay, that cannot be true, or why is it so popular?"

"Because good and generous emotions are more common to the human heart than we are aware till the appeal comes."

"Don't ask me to think that. I have found the world so base."

"Pardon me a rude question, but what do you know of the world?"

Beatrice looked first with surprise at Harley and then glanced round the room with significant irony.

"As I thought. You call this little room the world. Be it so. I will venture to say that if the people in this room were suddenly converted into an audience before a stage, and you were to deliver a speech full of sordid and base sentiments you would be hissed. But let any other woman, with half your powers, arise and utter sentiments sweet and womanly, or honest and lofty, and applause would flow from every lip and tears rush to many a worldly eye. The true proof of the inherent nobleness of our common nature is the sympathy it betrays with what is noble wherever crowds are collected. Never believe the world is base; if it were so no society could hold together for a day."

It may be that somewhat of awkwardness and crudity is developed in the personnel of our countrymen by the practical workings of our government that may be a little shocking to the sense of the fastidious.

But I never reflect upon the breadth and generosity of the underlying idea of our system of government, with all its manly equities, its constant demand upon its citizens for the most elevated sentiments known to our nature, and the opportunities afforded for their exercise, that it does not appear to me more and more, and beyond all other forms of government yet devised, the most favorable theatre for the exercise of all the qualities that dignify and adorn mankind, and that if penetrated with a true sense of the part which each man among us should bear in such a plan, an American citizen ought to be, in the best sense of the word, a gentleman.

I have had good reason to realize the exacting nature of the toil and varied occupation of our busy struggle in American life, and amid what a rush of events we have been carving civilization out of the wilderness, emulating with hot impatience the results and accumulations of centuries of work and thought in the older nations.

The graces of life — those fruits of repose and well-earned wealth and leisure — are of gradual growth, and have been necessarily postponed until our temple of civil and religious liberty should be erected upon secure foundations, and our grand experiment of self-control by a free people shall have been fully tested.

Art, its studies and higher influences, I do not underrate, and the great advantages it can impart to its disciples; but personal contact has taught me how much of that true refinement, delicacy of sentiment, and sensitive consideration for the feelings of others, which we justly regard as the best fruit of high breeding and culture, can and does exist in the simplicity of American society, uninstructed even by that European example which to some of our countrymen seems the necessary imprimatur of social success.

The roll would be a long one were I now to call the names of men born and bred under our Republican institutions, to praise whom would be but to echo feebly the applause which has resounded through the civilized world, who

> "Joined
> Each office of the social hour
> To noble manners, as the flower
> And native growth of noble mind."

When the manly and sound-hearted Thackeray scourged the petty pretenders and false livers of every rank in his own country, we read his "Book of Snobs" with keen satisfaction, and enjoyed the flagellation with which he visited social falsehood in his own land. And yet snobbishness, that wretched pinchbeck imitation of refinement and dignity, is, to my mind, venial in an Englishman, where it would be unpardonable in an American.

The American snob has none of the inducements or excuses of his British brother, and when he follows in his track, and gilds and veneers his pettiness and vulgarity in imitation of rank and distinguished station, he sins more against nature, and the honest simplicity and natural dignity which are akin to Republican institutions, and which may well be worn by every man who lives under them according to their true and manly spirit.

Self-respect is the basis of true personal dignity, and everything in the theory of our system tends to foster it.

It is in our power to create a standard of American character and manhood as lofty as that of any age or nation, and to compel our representatives at home and abroad to conform their conduct to it.

The spirit of true chivalry in all its gentleness and unselfishness, showing tenderness to the feeble and resistance to the overbearing, mercy to whom mercy is due, and honor to whom honor, can and does exist in America to-day, under the "hodden gray" of the laborer and mechanic, the thread-bare coat of the clerk, or the grave garb of the hard-worked merchant or man of the professions, as truly as it ever did under the helmet and chain-armor of any knight-errant in the olden time.

The American people can justly demand from those who are delegated to represent them abroad or at home a punctilious observance of honor and delicate pride in their private and public conduct, and the moral influence to be obtained by dignified self-respect, intelligence, and high personal integrity will far outweigh any attempted competition with the show and glitter of the representatives of other governments not based upon the principle of voluntary and orderly self-control.

In truth, it will be found that where American representatives abroad have drawn obloquy and just censure or contempt upon themselves or their country, it has been usually caused by some ignorant attempt at ostentatious display, or the unworthy pursuit of private gain, in both of which the dignity of their position was forgotten or disregarded, and the fault was not "Americanism," but the absence of it.

The self-assertion and acceptance of the unwritten law is necessarily exhibited in strong examples under the freedom of our system.

We profess to hold taxation without representation to be tyranny, and yet witness daily proofs that the most powerful influences upon society proceed from the unrepresented classes, of womanhood and infancy.

Few will deny the influence of the women of America upon public conscience and opinion, and the power they hold and exercise of moulding the national character. To woman is assigned the control of home and infancy, and from the gentle but mighty influences of her training comes what is most potential in men's lives.

All ideas, religious, moral, and political, must of necessity have their commencement and progress. It is a question of degrees; narrow and incomplete at first, they enlarge themselves and their influences insensibly until they reach the stage of public welfare.

The point of departure is the family, and under domestic influences the ideas are first nurtured; thence enlarging from the household to the State they soon proclaim themselves to the nation.

The unwritten law that gives the modesty and purity of American women such confessed control over public sentiment is recognized daily all over this broad land in the deference and respect paid everywhere to it in public.

Even in those regions of new discovery, where, tempted by the spirit of adventure, or the *auri sacra fames*, the roughest side of man's nature is developed, where the bowie-knife and revolver have a recognized authority and admitted jurisdiction, — even there, the presence of modest womanhood can still the oath or ribald song, and an unwritten law of American manhood obtains for delicacy and helplessness an homage as sincere and respectful as chivalry itself would exact.

With no other companion than modesty a woman may travel in any part of the United States, not only in safety but with an assurance of constant courtesy from men of every condition and with a possibility extremely remote of encountering incivility or insult.

As to the protection of legal rights of these two unrepresented classes, I could appeal to the experience of every practising lawyer in the land, whether the cause of the widow or the orphan has not a success before American juries, and sometimes judges as well, which can only be accounted for by the influence of supposed helplessness.

Property, *per se*, has no representation provided for it in the Federal Government, nor so far as I know in any of the States. During the continuance of negro slavery that "property" was recognized and favored by the Constitution, which gave a ratio of three-fifths representation to the communities which contained that description of persons. When that institution ended, representation of property in any form ceased to exist. Yet the power and influence of property and wealth in the government of this country is not only great but greatly to be dreaded, and mainly because it is not accompanied by open and well-defined responsibility.

Republican institutions have no worse foe than plutocracy, and the problem presented by the existence of those "artificial persons" called corporations, in their increasing number and power, in one of the most serious and difficult that confront this Government

Some one has said that "bribery is the revenge of property upon numbers," and so far as my knowledge goes its repression by statutes cannot be considered very effectual, and whenever it is checked and exposed it is by the unwritten law of home-bred honesty.

The excited and abnormal condition of political affairs in this country during the past ten years has given, perhaps unavoidably, an unusual conspicuousness to the military arm of the Government and invested its operations with a temporary importance which seems to have misled some people, and among them members of the army, in their estimate of the proper relations of the army of the United States to the people and their Government. The camp is a school in which opportunities for the study of the principles of civil government are but scantily afforded, and where the constructions of the Constitution and the administration of civil affairs are not apt to be closely considered.

"Martial law," said Sir Matthew Hale, "is not a law, but something indulged, rather than allowed, as a law. The necessity of government and discipline in an army is that only which can give it countenance."

"*Necessitas enim quod cogit defendit.*" I make this reference because of some remarks which have been lately going the rounds of the newspaper press and attributed to an officer of the highest rank in the army of the United States, who in publicly criticising and complaining of an alleged failure of Congress to make provision for the pay of the army, is reported to have said, in an after-dinner speech, " that *without the army the American people would be a mob.*"

It would be difficult in the same compass of words to confuse cause and effect more completely, or to conceive a more thoroughly un-American condition of mind than such a remark would seem to indicate.

Any government that depends for its peace and order upon a standing army is unworthy of the name of a free government of laws, and the sooner it gives way to another system the better for its inhabitants.

It is a fundamental principle in our system, that the military should be at all times, and strictly, subordinate to the civil authority; and this has been so often apparently overlooked or disregarded in the abnormal events of the last ten years, that we cannot be altogether surprised by the unconscious revelation of military misapprehension to which I have referred.

It is, however, one of the marks of the times, and should be noted, for it betrays a want of comprehension of the true principles upon which our Government was established, and under which alone it can be successfully maintained.

Let it never be forgotten that ours is wholly a voluntary system; that its true strength comes from the people, whose control is self-generated and is *from within;* and that for the use of mere coercive power, which governs us *from without,* we have no machinery of government whatever.

An examination of the constitutions of the General Government, and of the several States, will disclose no powers of which the will of the citizen is not a necessary element; that in our arrangement of political dynamics the popular will expressed under law is the sole motive-power.

The remark of the military officer I have quoted would place the creature above the creator, and imply that the instrument was more important than the power that constructed it, and by which it was guided.

Military unfitness for civil rule has often been exhibited, but no remark could better exemplify it.

The army of the United States, like the militia of the several States, is the creation of their respective legislation; like the " princes and lords " of Goldsmith's verse, —

"A breath can make them, as a breath hath made."

"He has kept among us, in times of peace, standing armies, *without the consent of the legislature,*" was one of the facts justifying revolution, "submitted to a candid world," by the founders of this Government. So long as human nature remains unchanged, the final argument of force cannot be disregarded; but, outside and beyond the will of the people expressed by law, an American army cannot exist: it is but their instrument for their own service. It is wholly dependent upon them; and they are never dependent upon it, and never will be while civil liberty exists in substance among us.

When called into existence, the army represents the military spirit of the whole nation, and is supported by the enthusiasm and pride of all. It is composed of American valor, skill, and energy, and is dedicated to the glory of our common country, whose history contains no brighter pages than those which record the naval and military achievements of her sons; but neither army nor navy stands now, nor ever did, nor ever will, towards the American people in the relation of policemen to a turbulent crowd. And those who would wish to see it placed in such an attitude, and employed in such work, are short-sighted indeed, and little regard the true dignity of the American soldier, or the real security of the American citizen.

The army of the United States is born of the martial spirit of a brave people, and is the product of national courage. This hall is hallowed as a memorial of the valor and devotion of those gallant youths who made themselves part of the army, at a time when they felt their country needed their service, and who freely offered up their lives upon the altar of patriotism.

"O, those who live are heroes now, and martyrs those who sleep."

Their surviving companions have returned to the paths of civil life, and the community is gladdened by their presence and strengthened by their example. If, to-morrow, the individuals who compose the army of the United States should return to the occupations of civil life, they would be quietly ingulfed in the great wave of humanity which rolls around them, and the true forces of the Government would move on in their proper orbits as quietly and securely as before the event.

Louis XIV. of France, "Le grand Monarque," —

of whom it was truly said "his highest praise was that he supported the stage-trick of royalty with effect,"—caused his cannon to be cast with the words, "Ultima ratio regum"; and his apothegm has so far advanced that in our day cannon seem, not the last, but the first and only, argument of royal government in Europe.

In the maze of strife, armed diplomacy, and exhausting warfare, in which all Europe now seems about to be involved, how just the picture drawn by Montesquieu nearly a century and a half ago!

"A new distemper has spread itself in Europe, infecting our princes, and inducing them to keep up an exorbitant number of troops. It has its redoublings, and of necessity becomes contagious; for as soon as one prince augments his forces the rest, of course, do the same, so that nothing is gained thereby but public ruin. Each monarch keeps as many armies on foot as if his people were in danger of being exterminated, *and they give the name of peace to this effort against all.*"

But a few weeks ago at Berlin, during a debate in the Imperial Parliament in relation to an increased grant of new captaincies of their army, a remarkable speech was made by General Von Moltke, that venerable master of the science of warfare. The telegram says: "He insisted on the necessity of the grant. He said he wished for long peace, but the times did not permit such hope. On the contrary, the time was not far distant when every government would be compelled to strain all its strength for securing its existence. The reason for this was the regretable distrust of governments towards each other. France had made great strides in her defences. Uncommonly large masses of troops were at present between Paris and the German frontier. Everything France did for her army received the undivided approval of her people. She was decidedly in advance of Germany in having her *cadres* for war ready in times of peace. Germany could not avoid a measure destined to compensate for it."

Will it not be well for Americans to comprehend fully the importance of the confession contained in this speech?

To-day the consolidated empire of Germany is confessedly the best organized and equipped military power on the globe.

To reach this end every nerve has been strained, every resource of that people freely applied. The idea of military excellence, like the rod of Aaron, has swallowed up all others; all others have bent to its service, until upon the shoulder of every man within her borders capable of bearing arms, the hand of the drill-sergeant has been laid, and from centre to circumference of the empire centralized military power reigns supreme.

Whatever of unqualified success a victory of arms can yield, surely it was achieved by Germany in her last memorable campaign against France. And history nowhere else exhibits in such completeness and precision the mathematical demonstration of successful scientific warfare.

With a rapidity and fulness scarcely credible, the student of history saw the "whirligig of time bring in his revenges," whilst the disciples of military art witnessed demonstrations of the problems of war executed upon a scale and with a steady and intelligible certainty that approached the marvellous.

Never was a military campaign more completely and at all points successful,— even to the conquest and dismemberment of the hostile territory as a safeguard for the future, and the exaction of enormous tribute by way of pecuniary reimbursement from the vanquished. Let us note well the fruit of it all, and learn so far as we may by the costly experience of others what are the consequences of such a system and policy. Does it secure peace, prosperity, and tranquil happiness? Let the victor answer.

It is Von Moltke, one of the chief architects of the system, himself who confesses, — even whilst the garlands of his great triumph are yet unfaded on his brow, — that he "longs for peace, but the times do not permit such hope. That every government is soon to be compelled to strain all its strength for securing its existence."

To the worshippers of military power and the believers in armed force as the chief instrumentality of human government I commend Von Moltke's speech.

If perfected military rule brings a people to such a pass, may Heaven preserve our country from it.

Well may we exclaim with the sightless apostle of English liberty, —

"What can war, but endless war still breed."

Even victory must have a future and the only victories which can have permanence, and the fruits of which grow more secure with time, are those of justice and reason; those of mere force are almost certain to contain self-generated seeds for their own subsequent reversal.

The safety and strength of our American Government consists in the self-reliant and self-controlling spirit of its people.

It was *their* courage, *their* intelligence, *their* virtues, that enabled our forefathers to build it up; and the same qualities and our sense of its value will inspire their descendants with love and courage to defend it.

> "Full flashing on our dormant souls the firm conviction comes.
> That what our fathers did for *theirs* — we would for *our* homes.

In 1789, no sooner was the original constitution of our Government adopted than the several States and their people hastened unanimously to declare in a second article of amendment that,

"A well-regulated militia being necessary to the security of a free state, the right *of the people* to keep and bear arms shall not be infringed."

And by Article 3d,

"No soldier shall, in time of peace, be quartered in any house without the consent of the owner; nor in time of war, but in a manner to be prescribed by law."

The right of THE PEOPLE to bear arms was thus sedulously guarded, and the necessary security of a free state was declared to be "a well-regulated militia." By the first article of the original Constitution, power was given to Congress to raise and support armies, but coupled with the express condition that no appropriation of money to that purpose should be made for a longer period than two years. When delegating power to Congress to call forth the militia to execute the laws of the Union, and suppress insurrection and invasion, the power was expressly reserved to the States, respectively, to appoint their own officers, and to train the militia according to the discipline prescribed by Congress.

Thus it will be seen that in the martial spirit of a free people, and in THEIR right to bear arms, the founders of our Government reposed their trust, and experience has proved how wisely.

The army of the United States is our honorable instrument of self-defence, and its organization, its numbers, its employment, are to be regulated wholly by law. The military is at all times to be subordinate to the civil authority, and dependent upon law for its powers, and the prescription of its duties.

The existence or non-existence of an army makes no change in the character or methods of our Government. It would be difficult to imagine a more unwarranted, and, to our American ear, more offensive statement than that "without the army the American people would be a mob."

The army and navy of the United States will be maintained in such strength as convenience, or the necessity of the Government, shall dictate; and they will be held in the respect and honor due to valiant and faithful public servants, but there must be no confusion in the public mind as to the nature and proper theatre of their duties, and their true relation to their fellow-citizens.

If erroneous ideas on this subject are beginning to take shape and find expression among us, let them be quietly but effectually discouraged.

Military force is always to be regarded with jealousy by a people who would be free.

It is only by military force that usurped power can have its pretensions enforced.

All history tells us that those who aspire to extraordinary power and dominion seldom trouble themselves about anything other than armies to enforce their pretensions, always decided by the possession of the longest sword.

And here, almost in the shadow of Bunker Hill, what words so befitting this grave topic, and the words of what man so proper to be recalled and heeded, as those of the patriot Webster, uttered four-and-thirty years ago, upon the completion of the monument there erected to the valor of the citizen-soldiers of America?

"Quite too frequent resort is made to military force; and quite too much of the substance of the people is consumed in maintaining armies, not for defence against foreign aggression, but for enforcing obedience to domestic authority. Standing armies are the oppressive instruments for governing the people in the ranks of hereditary and arbitrary monarchs.

"A military republic, a government founded on mock elections, and supported only by the sword, is a movement indeed, but a retrograde and disastrous movement, from the regular and old-fashioned monarchical systems.

"If men would enjoy the blessings of the republican government, they must govern themselves by reason, by mutual counsel and consultation, by a sense and feeling of general interest, and by an acquiescence of the minority in the will of the majority properly expressed; *and above all* the military must be kept, according to our bill of rights, in strict subordination to the civil authority.

"Wherever this lesson is not both learned and practised, there can be no political freedom. Absurd and preposterous is it, a scoff and satire on free forms of constitutional liberty, for frames of government to be prescribed by military leaders, and the right of suffrage to be exercised at the point of the sword."

The grandeur and glory of our Republic must have its base in the interests and affections of our whole people; they must not be oppressed by its weight, but must see in it the work of their own hands, which they can recognize and uphold with an honest pride, and which every emotion that influences men will induce them to maintain and defend.

They must feel in their hearts "the ever-growing and eternal debt which is due to generous government from protected freedom."

Silently and almost imperceptibly the generations succeed each other, and at the close of every third lustrum it is startling to mark what a new body of men have come into the rank of leadership in our public affairs.

How few of those who to-day guide and influence public measures did so fifteen years ago.

While it may not be in the power of leading men to control the decision of issues, it is in a great degree within their ability to create issues, by pressing forward subjects for public consideration; and herein lies much of the power of the demagogue, that pest of popular government, who, seeking only his own advancement, adroitly presents topics to the public calculated only to arouse their passions and prejudices, to the neglect of matters really vital.

Despite the almost perfect religious liberty in this country, the passions of sectarianism and the prejudices inseparable from such a subject are always to be discovered floating on the surface of society, ready to be seized upon by the shallow and unscrupulous.

The embers of such differences among mankind are never cold, and the breath of the demagogue can always fan them into flame, until the placid warmth of religion, instead of gently thawing the ice around human hearts, and imparting a glow of comfort to the homes of a happy community, becomes a raging conflagration in which the peace and good-will of society are consumed.

In a country so vast in its area, and differing so widely in all the aspects of life and occupation of its inhabitants, antagonism of interest, rivalry in business, and misunderstandings are frequently and inevitably to be expected; and the constant exercise of conciliation and harmony is called for to accommodate differences and soothe exasperation.

It is in the power of unscrupulous self seekers to raise such issues as shall involve, not the real interest and welfare of their countrymen, but their passions only, which are easily kindled, and can leave nothing but the ashes of disappointment and bitterness as the residuum.

The war between the good and evil influences in human society will never cease, and the champions of the former can never afford to lean idly on their swords, or slumber in their tents.

All around us we see successful men, vigorous and able, but unscrupulous and base, who have engraved success alone upon their banners, and as a consequence do not hesitate to trail them in the dust of low action, and stain them with disrepute, in pursuit of their object.

They keep within the pale of the written law, having its words on their lips, but none of its spirit in their hearts. Audacity and a self-trumpeting assurance are their characteristics. They reach a bad eminence, and contrive to maintain it, by all manner of self-advertisement; utterly immodest and indelicate, but successful in keeping themselves in the public eye. To them, politics is a mere game, in which stratagem and finesse are the means, and self-interest and personal advancement the end. Great aid is given to such characters by the public press, whose columns too often laud their tricky, shifty action, or at least give it the publicity it desires, without accompanying it with the condemnation it deserves.

How shall such influences be overcome? How shall we purge places of public station of men whose open boast is that they may be proven to be knaves, but cannot be called "fools"?

Nothing can effect this but the *unwritten law*, which shall create a tone of national honesty, truthfulness, and honor, to which the people will respond, and which will compel at least an outward imitation of the virtues upon which it is founded.

The armor of the Roman soldier covered only the front of his body. The cuirass shielded his breast, but his back was left unprotected. Each man felt himself to be the representative of the valor and good fame of his legion and his country.

The unwritten law of honor forbade him to turn his back upon danger, and thus became his impenetrable shield.

Such is the spirit and such are the laws that constitute the true safeguards of a nation against dangers from within and without.

What jurisdiction is more essential to be strictly and steadily maintained than that of *simple good faith*, which must extend everywhere, in every relation of life, and every phase of human existence? And what but an unwritten law, established by public conscience and opinion, can enforce its observance, or prescribe penalties for its breach?

The promptness and accuracy required in commercial transactions, the confidence and trust inseparable from them, would be fatally impeded if merchants had to depend only upon written statutes to protect them in their daily business, which needs and receives the ever present protection of the unwritten laws of commercial honor and integrity.

How insignificant is the proportion of those injuries which most affect our happiness, that can be prevented or punished by statute laws.

The laws of personal civility, of hospitality and social intercourse, are necessarily unwritten, but are not the less recognized and potential, and all these have consideration for the feelings and happiness of others as their motive-power,—imitations perhaps of the great and golden rule, "And as ye would that men should do unto you do ye also unto them in like manner."

These and countless others not capable of codification nor always of definition, are part of that fundamental system of law which must ever remain unwritten, and yet of which conscience and the opinions of mankind will take cognizance and to which they will ever render obedience. History will be read in vain to discover one act of fidelity and self-devotion, of high and generous self-sacrifice such as helped mankind in its performance and still helps them in its remembrance, that taught men to be better, purer, and more unselfish, that was not in obedience to the unwritten law.

No government is beyond the control of popular opinion, and nowhere is public opinion so direct and potential as under our system of universal suffrage. How essential, then, is it that this great agency should be based upon the unwritten laws of high intent and virtuous resolve! And who so capable of awakening and guiding these influences as the educated men of our country, and where should the appeal for their exertions be more successfully urged than here at this seat of sound learning and high culture?

Influence, *ex vi termini*, — *flows down upon* from above, and opinion and example must descend from the higher levels of thought and feeling with their influence.

If national tone and character depend, as we must believe they do, upon the popular education, — that is, the *drawing-out* of the people, — let us be careful as to what is so drawn out, and see to it that it is upon their better feelings and higher emotions alone that such draughts are made.

Upon the educated men of America a heavy responsibility rests for the condition of public opinion, as it is always in their power to contribute importantly to its formation.

The fact of their independence of public office and emolument gives them a greater influence in exempting them from suspicion of personal or party interests.

Cicero ranked beneficence by labor for the use of another as far higher than money gifts, which cost no trouble, and measured the favor by the sacrifice it cost to perform it.

The labor involved in diffusing and strengthening just opinions on public affairs among the masses of our countrymen, in battling with fallacies and frauds and their many advocates, is arduous indeed and never-ending.

But this is part of the obvious duty entailed upon the educated American, and from its performance he cannot, without discredit, escape.

And should he accept public office he will find it not

affording means and opportunities for luxury and enjoyment, but imposing important and sacred duties, which to a great extent will preclude attention from affairs of private interest and emolument. I am convinced that there is not another country in the world where a private citizen, unaided by official power, can exercise so beneficial an influence on his fellow-countrymen as in the United States. Nor can I imagine a more sublime aspiration than

> "That ere we fall in scattered fire
> Our hearts may lift the world's heart higher."

Throughout this country there are many such conscientious benefactors, quietly working for good government, and neither asking nor receiving any other reward than that which the sense of performed duty brings with it.

This land has been a theatre of high excitement and unhappy dissension, and on either side of the conflict the hearts of men have been stirred to their very depths, but in those depths how much that is worthy and noble and strong and sweet has been disclosed.

The record of the great armed struggle between the Northern and Southern sections of the Union developed on either side proofs of courage, self-devotion, magnanimity, and elevation of soul unsurpassed in history, that may justly fill us all with renewed pride, admiration, and respect for our national character.

And now it is, when the recognition of this mutual worth is taking place among our countrymen, when narrow distrust is giving way to just and generous confidence, when the smoke has lifted from the field, and clear and extensive views can be taken, that the time is so opportune to turn our minds from the vexatious squabbles and peevish controversies which have lately abounded, and join in the erection of a standard of American citizenship and public conduct around which the men of every State and every region of our country will gather with enthusiastic pride and affection.

Here let us raise it, everywhere in our family of States let it be raised, in the glad sunlight of liberty and law, of American brotherhood and heartfelt reconciliation!

It was related by Daniel Webster that on the day of his oration on laying the corner-stone of the monument at Bunker Hill, he called to see the venerable John Adams, and inquired as to his health. Said the aged patriot, "I inhabit a frail, weak tenement in decay; battered by the winds, and broken in upon by storms, and from all I can learn *the landlord does not intend to repair*."

Fellow-countrymen, this cannot be said of the temple of our political liberties, which has been rudely assailed and somewhat disfigured in its majestic architecture.

But our Great Landlord *does intend to repair*, and shall not we, his tenants, animated by a common impulse of gratitude, with hearts throbbing in patriotic unison, join with earnest and most willing hands in the glorious work and duty of strengthening the foundation, and rearing still higher, and in increased security and beauty, the fair fabric of American Constitutional Liberty?

To do this wisely the principles of its structure must be examined and studied, and, in the administration of its powers, never departed from.

If these poor words of mine shall have aided in such a work, and touched a responsive chord in your breasts, then I shall feel that my coming to you has not been in vain.

" Self-reverence, self-knowledge, self-control, —
These three alone lead life to sovereign power.
Yet not for power (Power of herself
Would come uncalled for), but to *live by law*,
Acting the law we live by without fear;
And because right is right, to follow right
Where wisdom is the scorn of consequence.'

Printed by Libri Plureos GmbH in Hamburg, Germany